You Will Get Sick

Noah Diaz

methuen | drama
LONDON • NEW YORK • OXFORD • NEW DELHI • SYDNEY

METHUEN DRAMA
Bloomsbury Publishing Plc, 50 Bedford Square, London, WC1B 3DP, UK
Bloomsbury Publishing Inc, 1359 Broadway, New York, NY 10018, USA
Bloomsbury Publishing Ireland, 29 Earlsfort Terrace, Dublin 2,
D02 AY28, Ireland

BLOOMSBURY, METHUEN DRAMA and the Methuen
Drama logo are trademarks of Bloomsbury Publishing Plc.

First published in the United States of America 2026
Copyright © Noah Diaz, 2026

Noah Diaz has asserted their right under the Copyright, Designs and Patents
Act, 1988, to be identified as author of this work.

For legal purposes the Acknowledgements on p. vii
constitute an extension of this copyright page.

Cover illustration and design by Megan Wilson

All rights reserved. No part of this publication may be: i) reproduced or
transmitted in any form, electronic or mechanical, including photocopying,
recording or by means of any information storage or retrieval system without
prior permission in writing from the publishers; or ii) used or reproduced in
any way for the training, development or operation of artificial intelligence
(AI) technologies, including generative AI technologies. The rights holders
expressly reserve this publication from the text and data mining exception
as per Article 4(3) of the Digital Single Market Directive (EU) 2019/790.

Bloomsbury Publishing Plc does not have any control over, or responsibility
for, any third-party websites referred to or in this book. All internet addresses
given in this book were correct at the time of going to press. The author and
publisher regret any inconvenience caused if addresses have changed or sites
have ceased to exist, but can accept no responsibility for any such changes.

No rights in incidental music or songs contained in the work are hereby
granted and performance rights for any performance/presentation
whatsoever must be obtained from the respective copyright owners.

All rights whatsoever in this play are strictly reserved and application
for performance etc. should be made before rehearsals to Creative Artists
Agency. No performance may be given unless a licence has been obtained.
No rights in incidental music or songs contained in the Work are hereby
granted and performance rights for any performance/presentation
whatsoever must be obtained from the respective copyright owners.

A catalogue record for this book is available from the British Library.

A catalog record for this book is available from the Library of Congress.

ISBN: PB: 978-1-3506-1872-5
ePDF: 978-1-3506-1873-2
eBook: 978-1-3506-1874-9

Series: Modern Plays

Typeset by Mark Heslington Ltd, Scarborough, North Yorkshire
Printed and bound in Great Britain

For product safety related questions contact
productsafety@bloomsbury.com.

To find out more about our authors and books visit
www.bloomsbury.com and sign up for our newsletters.

You Will Get Sick originally opened off Broadway at Roundabout Theatre Company's Harold and Miriam Steinberg Center for Theatre/Laura Pels Theatre where it ran from October 14 to December 11, 2022 with the following cast and creative team.

1	Daniel K. Isaac
2	Linda Lavin
3	Marinda Anderson
4	Nate Miller
5	Dario Ladani Sanchez
u/s 1	Daniel Liu
u/s 2	Becca Lish
u/s 3	Bianca Horn
u/s 4, 5	Bobby Roman
Playwright	Noah Diaz
Director	Sam Pinkleton
Scenic Design	dots
Costume Design	Michael Krass and Alicia Austin
Lighting Design	Cha See
Sound Design	Lee Kinney
Hair Design	Tommy Kurzman
Original Music	Daniel Kluger
Illusions	Skylar Fox
Dramaturg	Madeline Charne

You Will Get Sick ran in Steppenwolf Theatre's Downstairs Theatre from June 5 to July 20, 2025 with the following cast and creative team.

1	Namir Smallwood
2	Amy Morton
3	Sadieh Rifai
4	Cliff Chamberlain
5	Jordan Arredondo
u/s 1	Dennis Renard
u/s 2	Meighan Gerachis

u/s 3	Stephanie Shum
u/s 4	Carl Lindberg
u/s 5	Alex Benito Rodriguez
Playwright	Noah Diaz
Director	Audrey Francis
Scenic Design	Andrew Boyce
Costume Design	Raquel Adorno
Lighting Design	Jen Schriever
Sound Design	Willow James
Vocal Coach	Kate DeVore
Illusions	Skylar Fox
Dramaturg	Bryar Barborka

SICK

GET

WILL

YOU

Who

1, man, 30s
2, woman, 70s or older
3, woman, 30s
4, man, 30s or 40s
5, man, 20s or younger

Actors 1, **3**, *and* **5** *are non-homogeneous actors of color*
Actors 2 *and* **4** *are white*

Where

The Big City

When

A time before cell phones

How

Actor 5 isn't seen, until he is
He speaks into a microphone, until he doesn't

Narrated lines are set in *italics*
Stage directions are centered in (parentheses)

There are very few pauses or interruptions in this play

For my uncle-in-law, who got sick

&

For my aunt, who was there for him when he did

1

1
I can pay you twenty dollars

5
the connection on the telephone crackles, just a little bit

1
Is that okay?

2
Your flyer said forty

5
you can hear her breathing

1
I know

5
you have asthma

her breathing makes you wonder if she has asthma too

1
But I tried to cross it out with a marker

2
Yeah, I saw that you tried to cross it out
but it said forty

1
I can pay you twenty

5
the telephone crackles again, just a little bit

and then it's quiet

*but you can still hear her breathing
so you know she's still there*

1
Hello?

2
This a sex thing?
I don't wanna listen to you jerk off

1
No
I just need to tell you something

2
And then we hang up?

1
Yeah

2
And then you'll mail me a check?

1
Yeah, but I can only pay you twenty dollars

2
Can you send it to my school?
The main office has a box for uh
for student mail

1
Oh

2
I don't wanna give you my address

5
a bird caws outside your window

it's too tremendous, too prehistoric
too loud for a city this big

the sound fills your apartment

2
Hello?

5
and then it's quiet

1
Yeah, that's fine

2
Box 1816365
Temple Royale Community College
The Eighth Avenue location

1
Okay

2
Did you write it down?

1
I'll remember it

2
Repeat it back to me

1
Box 1816365
Temple Royale Community College
The

1 *and* **2**
Eighth Avenue location

2
Good
So what is it?

1
I'm just supposed to –?

2
Your flyer said you wanted someone to call you

1
Right

2
So what is it?

5
you breathe

you wonder if she wonders if you have asthma
you want to tell her that you do

2
Hello?

5
but you don't

1
I'm nervous

2
Jesus Christ
We gonna do this or not?
Because I've got a

5
you tell her everything

and it hurts just as much as you thought it would

but you do it

and then you're done

and you don't feel better
but you do feel different

1
That's it

5
the phone doesn't crackle

you don't hear her breathe

there's just quiet

and the sound of a big bird flapping its wings outside your window

1
Thanks for listening

5

you hang up

and you write the check

you think you hear a bird caw again

further now
blocks away

2

5

that night you take a shower
and you imagine her

whoever she is

in a community college
in a night class

standing at a podium
in front of people she doesn't really know
and who don't really know her

2

My project partner is out sick
Something about bad water pressure in her shower
or maybe it was bad water itself
Like bacteria or something
I don't know
I couldn't make out what she was saying over the phone
But she has the uh
the slides we were going to use
so
So I guess I'll just share some of the notes we took?
I have those somewhere
Uh
okay
We were assigned the neighborhoods between Seventy-First
and Forty-Third

just between the park with the pack of wild dogs and that bodega with all the cats in it
We uh
we titled our project Gentrification And How It's Effected The Neighborhoods Between Seventy-First and Forty-Third, Just Between The Park With The Pack of Wild Dogs And That Bodega With All The Cats In It
which, okay yeah
Now that I read that out loud
that's
not great
And I spelled Affected wrong
so
That's not great either
My partner and I explored the neighborhoods, and we talked to some of the people who live there
I met this lady who sleeps in the park and takes care of the wild dogs
She told me this story about how she was trying to open a can of raviolis for her husband and suddenly the sky got dark, like a shadow was covering the entire city
And then a crow, this big ass crow
the size of a house or something
swoops down and snatches the old man in its beak
She said it happened so quickly
One second, husband
Next second, no husband
Next second, sun
Next second, a man screaming somewhere in the clouds
So that's weird, right?

5

the clarifying shampoo stings your eye

1
Ow

2
We only split up once

She wanted to knock on doors in this housing complex for midgets
Wait, little people?
Little midgets?
I forget what we're supposed to say
She wanted to talk to the little midget people, but I wanted to keep walking, so we split up
I walked past townhouses
and parks
and bodegas
and past an old factory that makes beepers
Everything looks gentrified, so I'm feeling good, right?
But then
I get to the very edge of our assigned area, right on the corner of Forty-Third
and I see a telephone pole with a flyer on it that says
Wanted:
Someone To Call Me
I Need To Tell You Something I'm Not Ready To Tell Anyone I Know
I Will Pay You Forty Dollars
but the forty part is scratched out with marker and rewritten to say twenty, but you can still see forty
So I call the number because I could really use twenty or forty bucks or whatever
and this guy answers
and he tells me that he's been falling a lot lately
His balance isn't right
and his smile keeps getting stuck all crooked
He gets nervous looking at it in the mirror because it doesn't curve up the right way anymore
His doctor says he's sick
and that it's not good
I guess it's
uh
it's actually pretty bad
His body is
is

I don't know
It's failing him
But there are things that can help until it gets worse
Which it will
Get worse, I mean
Then the guy says he's very scared and very sad
and he thanks me for listening and then he hangs up
The check he sends is for one hundred dollars
and the memo part says: Thanks For Listening
So
that's weird too, right?

5

and maybe that's exactly how it happens

or maybe it isn't

3

2
You didn't sign it

5
the connection on the telephone crackles again, just a little bit

1
Sign what?

2
The check

5
your left hand crackles too

2
You didn't sign the check

1
Yes, I did

2
No, you didn't

1
I know I did because

2
I'm looking at it right now
I thought they'd let me cash it anyways, but they won't

1
Oh

2
Can you send another one?

1
I don't have any more

2
You don't have to lie

1
I'm not lying

2
Yes, you are

1
I'm not

2
I'm an actor
I know when people are lying

1
You're a what?

2
You blinked when you said it
We call that a giveaway

1
We're on the telephone

2
I can tell you blinked

1
Through the receiver?

2
Yep

1
Okay, what am I doing now?

        (**Actor 1** *holds his middle finger to the receiver*)

2
Yeah, fuck you too

        (**Actor 1** *looks behind himself, just in case*)

2
Listen, I know you blinked and I know you're lying, and that's whatever, okay?
I just want

1
Maybe my face was having a spasm

2
What?
No
Don't do that

1
Do what?

2
Don't pull that sick shit with me

1
I could've spasmed

2
You could've, but you didn't

1
I have a lot of spasms

2
And I have a lot of things to do today, so can you just cut me another check?

5
your hand goes numb

2
Please
It's one hundred dollars

5
you rub it

2
That's
a lot of money

5
you shake it

2
It's money I could use

1
I thought I signed it

2
You didn't

1
My brain

5
your right hand goes numb too

2
Listen
I called you, didn't I?

5
you hold the phone to your shoulder

1
Yeah

5
rubbing your hands together

2
You told me what you had to say
and I listened to you
so that means I should get paid, right?

5
you try to rub the numb away

1
Right, but

5
the phone shifts

2
I'll take forty

5
it slips

2
Twenty

5
it falls to the floor

2
I'll just take twenty like the flyer said

5
you try to pick it up

2
Hello?

5
but you can't

2
Hello?

5
your hands are too numb

2
I know this is
I know it's weird

5
they crackle too much

2
C'mon
I'm sorry for saying you lied

5
you lie on the floor

2
Are you there?

5
your ear to the phone

2
Please

5
your hands still crackling

2
I have some things I need to pay for
I have a

1
Hey
sorry
I
It's my sister's checkbook

2
What?

1
Her name's on the check

2
Oh fuck
Yeah

1
I closed my checking account when I got
uh
you know
So she gave me some checks and I paid her in cash

5
and then it's quiet

for a very long time

1
I have asthma

2
So do a lot of people

1
Do you?

5
she puffs an inhaler

2
No

1
I dropped the phone

2
Then pick it up

1
I can't

2
Why?

1
My hands
My grip
I don't know

2
That part of it?
The –?

1
I guess so

2
Bummer

5
you can hear her breathing

you're becoming familiar with its rhythm

2
I'm sorry for calling
I'll just
try another bank, see if they can

1
I have some cash

2
You do?!

1
Yeah

2
Great!
How much?

1
Enough to give you one hundred
But I want the check back

2
Can I get it today?

1
Oh, well, I

2
I could meet you before my class!

1
I can just mail it to you

2
No, I'll meet you

1
Sure
Sure, if that's

2
How about the telephone pole on the corner of Forty-Third?
The one with your flyer

1
Okay

2
Okay?

1
Okay

2
Okay!

4

4
Quick!
Easy to sign up!
Low deductibles!
Get your certified bird insurance today!

5
a man is standing beneath your telephone pole

4
There's no time to waste, folks!
Who knows when a giant bird will swoop down and swallow you whole!
Ensure your coverage by insuring with me!

5
a cardboard cutout of a bird hides your flyer

4
Low premiums!
No out-of-pocket expenses!
Just guaranteed protection from gargantuan birds!

5
he slips a knife from his pocket

and stabs the bird over and over
and over again

4
When Mr. Gently has your back, the world is a gentler place!

5
he tries to pass a stack of flyers your way,
but they seem to catch flight

taking to the wind, traveling everywhere but your hand

4
Here!

5
he's in front of you

1 (*startled*)
Fuck

5
pressing a business card into your chest

4
I can't promise it won't kill you
but I can promise that it won't hurt when it does

1
Excuse me?

4
The sick inside you

1
I'm not

4
I can smell it

1
What?
No!
I

4
Take the card
Give me a ring

2
Leave him alone

5
it's her

1
It's you

5
you don't know when she appeared or how

2
Go hock your bullshit on some other corner

5
the man leans into you

4
Mr. Gently can make it gentler
I can promise you that

2
Goodbye!

4 (*to* **2**)
If he's not interested, are you?
Special time offer
Low premiums
No out-of-

2
I said goodbye!

4
You know what they say about the uninsured
Bad luck always hits 'em first
Life's like that, ya know

2
Great, thanks, fuck off

4
Eat me, lady

2
I want a meal, not a snack

5
he gives you a wink

and then he's gone

2
Do you have the cash?

1
Maybe I should've gotten insured

2
Go somewhere more reputable
You don't want bird insurance from him
Do you have the cash?

1
Yeah
Do you have the check?

2
Yeah

1
Good

2
Give it to me

1
Give me the check

2
Give me the cash

1
Give me the check

2
Give me the cash

1
I wanna see the check

2
I wanna see the cash

                    (**Actors 1** *and* **2** *stare at each other*)

        (*and then slowly reach into their pockets at the same time*)

5
your hands shake

but at least they don't crackle

2
It's the full one hundred?

1
I only had small bills

2
Thanks

1
Sure

5
you begin to cough

2
I really appreciate this

1
What are you doing with it?

2
I don't think that's any of your business

5
you can't stop coughing

1
It's my money

2
No, it's not

1
It came from my pocket

2
And it's going into mine
Stop coughing

1
I can't

2
Pinch your nose

1
What?

2
Just try

5
you do

you try

1
It hurts

2
Wait

5
you do

you wait

and then you slowly stop coughing

2
See

1
Thanks

5
you peer at each other

and then suddenly

>(**Actor 2** *starts to sing the first lines of Somewhere Over the Rainbow*)
>
>(*she suddenly stops mid-phrase, out of breath*)
>
>(**Actor 2** *puffs an inhaler*)

2
Did that sound good?

1
No

2
Really?

1
You went too low on the Way part of Way Up High

2
Fuck
I keep doing that

5
you're suddenly very lonely

you want to tell her this

2
Okay bye

5
but you don't

1
What are you doing today?

2
I don't date sick people

1
I don't date women, but that's not what I asked

2
Oh
I have class at seven

1
I'm having lunch with my sister

2
Okay?

1
I'll give you twenty bucks to tell her that I'm
that I'm

2
Sick?

1
Yeah

2
One-twenty

1 (*an eyeroll*)
Fuck you
Fifty

2
Seventy-five

1
Fifty

2
Fifty and you buy my lunch

1
Okay

2
Fifty, lunch, and then a dessert

1
Fine

2
And you be my scene partner in class tonight
Great, let's go!

1
Wait!

2
Please!
My partner is still out sick
I need someone to fill in or we won't have an even rotation of people

1
What do I have to do?

2
Just
I don't know

Make it up as you go!
Just exist inside your body
That's all

5

you're not sure

2

Please

1

Fine, but I'm not buying you a dessert then

2

We'll see

5

she turns the corner, walking toward the train

2

By the way, you've got something in your hair

5

you run your hand along your head

and some hay falls to the ground

5

4

Welcome to Burger Bang, where you get a better bang for your burger buck!

5

it looks like your waiter has been crying

4

I'm Rosco
I'll be serving you this afternoon
Can I get you folks anything to drink?

5

you want to ask him why

but your mouth won't let you

1
My mouth

2
You okay?

1
It's

5
hard to speak

2
What?

5
your tongue is

1
Dry

2
Water
You need some water?
(*to* **4**)
Get him some water

4
Okie doke!

5
you start to cough again

you try to pinch your nose

3
There he is!

5
your sister is striding towards you

her shoes clack on the tile

3
What're you doing?
Stop it

5
you're getting dizzy

2
Rosco's getting him some water

5
your hands start to crackle

3
Who's Rosco?

5
your legs crackle too

3
Who're you?

5
and then
you cough up some hay

3
Ew!
What the fuck is that?!

1
Hay

3
Hi
What is that?

1
It's hay

3
Oh
Don't do that again

5
you puff an inhaler

1
Hi, Polly

3
Who is she?

2
Callan

1
She's

4
Here we go!
Two waters!

5
your waiter's trying not to cry

4
Oh shoot, I'm sorry, I
I didn't see your third come in

5
he spins around

4
Goddamn you, Rosco!

>   (**Actor 4** *slaps himself across the face*)

5
and then he's back

4
Welcome to Burger Bang, where you can bang a burger for your burger bucks!
I'm Rosco
Can I get you something to –?

3
Diet whatever with lime

4
Can I interest anyone in an appetizer?
Our Bang-Bang Burger Basket is

3
No, but that diet whatever with lime would be so great, thank you

4
Okie doke!

5
and then he's gone

your sister looks between you and your new acquaintance

3
I didn't know we were bringing friends today

2
We're not friends

3
No?

2
Nope

3
Then why are you here?

2
Business

5
your sister glances at you

she presses her toe into your foot

3
You work with my brother?

1
Kind of

3
So you're in –?

2
Show business
I'm an actor

3
No, I meant

2
Stage mostly
I'm taking night classes at a community college
I'm in one right now called Body as Source
We're learning how to live inside our bodies
I'm getting better at it

3
You pay tuition for that?

1
It sounds interesting
Learning how to live inside yourself
That might be really
useful

5
you realize that you can't feel your sister's toe anymore

your leg has gone numb

4
Diet whatever with lemon!

3
Lime!

(**Actor 4** *sobs*)

4
Are we ready to order?

3
No

4
Okie doke!

5
and then he's gone

3
I'm

5
your sister peers at the stranger at your table

3
Confused
What're you doing here?

2
Here?

3
Here-here

2
Oof
Here-Here
Going straight for the big questions, huh?
Well, I guess I'm still figuring it out
I'm seeing how this acting thing goes, but I'd be hesitant to call it my capital P purpose, you know?

3
Is she fucking with me?

1
No, I think she's

2
I'm taking these classes
I'm reading the books
I'm doing good work and I feel like the training's there

but none of the auditions I've been on have led to anything, so

3
Hey!
I'm asking why you're sitting at this table with my brother and I

2
Oh

3
Right

2
Okay
He's paying me to tell you something
Wanna do it now or should we wait to order?

3
What?

4
Here I am!

5
your waiter's really crying now

his shirt is wet with tears

4
Have we decided on what we'd –?

3
Burgers!

4
Okie doke!

2
I actually wanted a

5
but he's gone, and you can hear his crying echo in the kitchen

3
What is this?

5
you can hear it all the way from there

3
This an ambush?

1
It's nothing, Polly, it's

3
Who is she?

1
Calm down
It's not a big deal

3
Don't do that
I hate when you do that

1
Do what?

3
Tell me to calm down!
You know that just upsets me even more

1
There's nothing to be upset about

3
You brought a *stranger* to lunch

2
I called the number on his ad and now he

3
His *what*?

2
His ad
His flyer

3
Your *flyer*?!

1
I made a flyer asking someone to call me because I had some some
some news I wanted to practice saying out loud and

3
So you called her?!

1
Well, no, she called me

3
I'm your sister!
I'm
Okay, you know what?
I *am* going to calm down because my suitcase is full, and I

2
Your what?

3
My *suitcase*
I don't have enough room to carry around someone else's issues, okay?
My bag is full

2
What suitcase?

3
My Metaphorical Suitcase, bitch!

1
Polly, honey, just take a breath
You don't even know what the

3
I don't know why you do this to me
It's like you *want* to stress me out

2
Your sister's a pill

3
What did you just say?

2
I said you're a pill

1
Callan

3
You don't even know me

2
I've seen enough to take a good guess

3
I hope a bird gets you

2
Good one

3
I hope it's the sickest fucking bird out there

2 (*to* **1**)
I'm just trying to eat and get to class
Should I tell her or not?

3
Tell me what?!
(*to* **1**) Why won't you –?!

2
Your brother is sick

5
the table gets very, very quiet

you can hear your waiter's sobs

they echo through the restaurant

3
He's what?

5
suddenly
you can feel your leg again

3
You're what?

2
He's sick
His body is sick and it's not good
He was scared to tell you, so he paid me to do it
And by the way, I wanted to order a grilled chicken Buck Buck Bite

5
your sister lays her head on the table

and she doesn't say anything
for a very long time

3
I'll take care of you

1
Polly

3
I'll learn how

1
It's

3
You took care of Patrick

2
Patrick?

1
Brother

3
It's my turn now
I'll take care of you

1
No

3
I can do it
I can

1
No, honey

(**Actor 1** *sighs*)

1
I know you want to
But no

5
the table gets very quiet again

3
Will you do the thing?

1
The –?

3
Patrick's thing, yeah
I
I want to touch you right now, but I know you don't like it
so please
I need you to do the thing
I

1
Okay

Yeah
Sure

5
you lift your hand
and crack an egg on your sister's head

>   (**Actor 1** *"cracks an egg" on* **Actor 3***'s head**)

5
you stay like that for a while

1
Things just happen

5
you can hear your sister breathe
facedown on the table, your hand in her hair

1
I'll make it through

5
she lifts her head, and you see that she's been crying

3
Does it hurt?

1
No

5
you lie

1
It doesn't hurt at all

5
she begins to flip through an address book

3
Maybe the agency we used for Patrick has a branch here in

---

* *This gesture is three gentle taps of an egg-shaped fist on the top of the head before letting the fingers "crack" and run through the hair like yolk.*

the city
I'll see if I can find someone to help out

1

I don't want someone moving in with me

3

They don't have to move in
They have levels or packages or something
We can find someone to stop in every now and then, just to check on you

1

Listen to me
I'm telling you that I don't want someone
Not every day, not every now and then, not at all
I don't want someone

3

Well, I

2

He doesn't want someone

3

Well, I don't give a fuck what he wants
I can't watch another one of my brothers get sick
I can't
I can't
I'll take care of it

5

she's standing

3

Bathroom?

1

Back left corner

5

and then she's gone

her shoes clacking on the tile

4
Here we go, folks!

5
you have a different waiter now

4
Three Big Bang Bronco Burgers

5
he's older, more tired, as if he's seen the world

1
What happened to Rosco?

4
Had to send him home
He got word that his mom was taken by a bird
He was upsetting the customers

1
Oh

4
Should've gotten her insured
But life's like that, ya know?
Shoulda coulda woulda

2
Yeah, hey
Can I switch my burger for a grilled chicken Buck Buck Bite?

6

3
Now begin walking around the room

5
everyone begins to walk around the classroom

*you watch them for a moment
and then you begin to walk too*

your leg cramps, but you keep moving

3
Now imagine you're a lion
Walk like a lion!

5
*your new friend who isn't really a friend but more like a business
associate walks like a lion*

you try to walk like a lion too

3
Good!
Good work, folks!
Slowly transition out of lion
Great
Now begin to walk like a tiger

2
Lion and tiger feel very similar to me, Teacher Taylor

3
Stay in it, Callan

2
But

3
Just do it
Okay, everyone, keep tiger-ing!

5
your leg spasms

but you try to walk like a tiger

3
Beautiful!

5

you try your very best

3

I love what I'm seeing!

> (**Actor 2** *roars like a tiger*)

3

No character work

2

Got it

3

Slowly transition out of tiger
Good
Beautiful
Let's see some bears

5

your leg goes numb

1

I can't

3

There is no *can't*
There is only *try*

2 *and* **3** *and* **4**

We call that *do*

1

What?
What does that even mean?

3

Okay, let's try one more!
I'll do this one with you
Walk like you're so sick a bird is about to take you

> (**Actors 2**, **3**, *and* **4** *walk like they're sick*)

you watch them for a moment
and then you begin to walk too

your leg cramps, but you keep moving

3
Now imagine you're a lion
Walk like a lion!

5
your new friend who isn't really a friend but more like a business associate walks like a lion

you try to walk like a lion too

3
Good!
Good work, folks!
Slowly transition out of lion
Great
Now begin to walk like a tiger

2
Lion and tiger feel very similar to me, Teacher Taylor

3
Stay in it, Callan

2
But

3
Just do it
Okay, everyone, keep tiger-ing!

5
your leg spasms

but you try to walk like a tiger

3
Beautiful!

5
you try your very best

3
I love what I'm seeing!

> (**Actor 2** *roars like a tiger*)

3
No character work

2
Got it

3
Slowly transition out of tiger
Good
Beautiful
Let's see some bears

5
your leg goes numb

1
I can't

3
There is no *can't*
There is only *try*

2 *and* **3** *and* **4**
We call that *do*

1
What?
What does that even mean?

3
Okay, let's try one more!
I'll do this one with you
Walk like you're so sick a bird is about to take you

> (**Actors 2**, **3**, *and* **4** *walk like they're sick*)

(**Actor 1** *walks without affectation*)

3
And slowly
transition
out
of
sick
Great!
Fantastic warm-up, everyone!
Thanks for your commitment

2
Teacher Taylor, are we –?

4 (*loudly*)
What was that?!
I'm still coming out of sick!

(**Actor 4** *shakes off his actorly sickness*)

2 (*an eyeroll*)
I said *Teacher* Taylor, not *Student* Taylor
(*to herself*) Asshole
(*to* **3**) Are we going to work on voice tonight, Teacher Taylor?
My audition is next week and I'm still going low in my song

3
I can see if we have time at the end of class, but we've got a lot to get through

2
Can I stay after and go over it with you?

3
Thirty bucks

2
Ten

3
Twenty-five

2
Fifteen

3
Twenty

2
Deal

3
Okay, everyone, let's get started!
Let's turn inward tonight and focus on our interior lives
I want to examine all the parts that make you You
What's squiggling around in your guts?
What's in there right now that we can use for your art?

5
you touch your body

you wonder where the sick is right this very second

3
We'll start with partner work
Frankie's out sick, so we have an odd number for rotations
Two of you, pair up!

4
Hey!

5
he's in front of you

4
Welcome to class!

5
he smiles

you want to tell him that he looks like someone you used to love

1
You look like someone I

4
You've seen my work?!

5
but you don't

1
No

4
Damn

3
Tell your partner a secret

4
This one's fun

1
What do I –?

4 (*a loud whisper*)
I have a paralyzing fear of open spaces

3
Now let it live inside your body

                      (**Actor 4** *performs*)

5
you watch him

and you marvel at how he's able to live inside his body

                      (**Actor 4** *stops performing*)

4
Now you go

1
Oh

5
give it a try

1
Okay

4
Use your breath

1
I'm

4
And your body

1
I'm

5
there you go

4
Stay grounded

1
I'm very

      (**Actor 1** *can't bring himself to say it*)

5
it's okay

you don't have to say it

1
I can't think of a secret

3
Switch partners!

2
He's so annoying, right?
Did he say anything about my monologue from last week?

1
What?
No
You were right there

3 (*to* **1** *and* **2**)
Tell each other what you really *want*
Dig way down deep

1
I want to go home

2
What? No!
Class just started!
You promised
I told your sister for you, so you have to stay

1
No, I meant

2 (*solemnly*)
I want to play Dorothy

1
You what?

2
I have an audition for *The Wizard of Oz* next week

1
Dorothy Dorothy?

2
Yeah

1
The twelve-year-old farmgirl?

2
Judy Garland was seventeen when she filmed the movie

1
And you think you look seventeen?

2
Great actors can do anything
They can play any age

1
Right
Did this Dorothy see the trials of war and age sixty years?

2
Funny

1
Did she peer into the Ark of the Covenant and melt?

2
This classroom is a safe space
You can't make fun of

    (**Actor 2** *puffs an inhaler*)

2
What I want, asshole

3
Okay!
I need a pair to work with in front of the group

2
We'll do it!

3
Great!

1
What are we –?

2
Shut up, we're doing this

5
you stand in the center of the room

you can feel your leg begin to cramp again

3
Face each other

5
you try to shake it off

3
Now tell each other what you want

1
I want

3
No no
Tell each other with the body

> (**Actor 1** *and* **Actor 2** *begin to silently perform**)

5
it becomes a little more graceful as you both go along

a little more real

a little more true

3
And begin to bring it to a close
Wow
Great work
Let's take a breather, folks

5
you breathe

she breathes

you both puff on your inhalers

7

5
that night you take a shower
and you imagine her

in a community theater
in an audition

---

* *This moment of physicality can manifest in so many different ways, but it shouldn't be played comedically.*

standing on an empty stage
in front of a crowd of giant birds

2
Hello
My name is Callan
I'll be auditioning for the role of Dorothy in your production
of *The Wizard of Oz* based on the 1939 film of the same
name
I have prepared for you a song and a monologue
I will begin with the song
Thank you

                (**Actor 2** *takes a breath*)

2 (*starts to sing the first lines of Somewhere Over the Rainbow*)

                (**Actor 2** *stops*)

2 (*out of breath*)
Okay that's it

5
she puffs an inhaler

2
I will now perform a monologue written by some guy I met

                (**Actor 2** *takes a breath*)

2
I started falling last month
My legs would go numb and they'd
I don't know
they'd just give out on me
I'd rub them
I'd keep rubbing them until I got the feeling back
But then I noticed it in my face
It was going numb too
I couldn't smile right
It'd curve up on the left but that's all it would be able to do
My

my mom says I have a nice smile
I think about that
How I won't be able to smile at my mom the right way
anymore
I tried chewing gum
sucking on mints
eating taffy
I thought it would be like rubbing my leg, but doing it on the inside of my mouth, you know?
And it usually kind of worked, but sometimes it wouldn't, so I'd just be sitting there with green apple taffy stuck in my throat because I couldn't make my body swallow it
I finally had to call my neighbor because I woke up one morning and my arm was limp
Stayed limp for six hours
I couldn't move it
He drove me to the emergency room because we thought I had a stroke
The doctor did some tests, and when she finally came into the room, she said that it's
uh
it's not good
It's actually quite bad
She gave my neighbor some paperwork to take home with me
but it's mostly just stuff on how to ease the pain
There's nothing they can really do to fix it
It's a uh
a time thing

5
you breathe

2
I could manage it
My body failing me
It
it was hard, but I could manage it
But then one night I was on the train home and I couldn't

remember which stop was mine
I sat there for twenty minutes trying to remember
and maybe I missed my stop or maybe I didn't, but I just
I
I couldn't remember
So I leaned over to the guy next to me and I said, "Did I miss my stop?"
And he said, "Which stop is yours?"
I didn't say anything because I got scared
So he said, "Where you going?"
And I said, "Home"
And he said, "Where's that?"
And I stared at him
and he stared at me
and we stared at each other
and I told him the truth
I said, "I don't know"
And that's when I realized that it was in my brain

5
she breathes

2
It had gotten its way up there
So that's a
uh
A different set of circumstances, I think
Right?
I
Yeah
So
you're calling me so I can tell you
that I'm

5
you breathe together

2
That I'm sick
My body is sick

My mind is
is
is probably getting sick too
And it makes me sad
and angry
and prematurely tired because I know that I'm going to have to keep telling people what's happening to me over and over and over again
But I'm
I'm getting better at saying it
So
That's it
Thank you for listening

      (**Actor 2** *bows*)

2
Thank you

5
and then suddenly

your leg goes limp
and you fall
hitting your head with a hard crack

you can't move it

you think you can hear a giant bird flying above your head

but maybe it's only the roar of the shower

or maybe you're just imagining it

     (**Actor 1**'s *leg is different now*)

      (*it's a different texture or fabric*)

       (*it's stuffed with hay*)

8

2
You're what?

5
*the connection on the telephone doesn't crackle
but her voice sounds distant*

1
On the floor

2
Get up

1
I can't

2
Did you fall?

1
Yeah

2
Where?

1
The shower

2 (*a tsk*)
Slippery

5
you try to rub your leg

1
I don't think my leg is coming back

2
Why're you calling me?

1
Will you take me to Twenty-First and Metropolitan Avenue?

There's a place around there that sells like
canes and wheelchairs and stuff

2
How much?

1
Eighty

2
Two-fifty

1 (*an eyeroll*)
Sixty

2
Sixty, but in cash

1
Deal

9

2
This one looks good
It has four little rubber things on the end

5
she's holding two canes
one in each hand

2
But this one has an extender thing, just in case you start to
hunch over and need to shorten it

1
Whoa, wait

5
you're sitting in a display wheelchair

your leg hangs limp to the side

1
You think my body's going to hunch?

2
I mean
Yeah
Probably

1
I wonder if I shouldn't just get a wheelchair
I don't think my other leg is strong enough to drag this one along

2
Looks like there's a bundle deal right now
Buy a chair for three-twenty-five and get a cane for thirty bucks

5
she eyes your leg

2
Might want to take them up on that

3
Omigod!

5
a woman is striding toward you on two strong legs

3
Hi, you!

5
you impulsively try to stand

3
Aren't those fun?!

I was rolling around the store in one last week when I was shopping for my dad

1
They're

fun, yeah
Callan, this is uh
Margot, a coworker of mine
Callan is a
She's

2

A business associate

3

Oh, okay!
Ew, you've got something on your

> (**Actor 3** *pulls hay out of* **Actor 1**'s *shoulder as she speaks*)
>
> (**Actor 1** *winces in pain*)

3

So where have you been?
You haven't been in the office in so long!
I didn't realize you had that much time saved up

1

I've been a little under the weather

3

Yeah, it's that time of the year
Let me know if you need anything
I know a fantastic ear-nose-and-throat guy

1

I'll do that, thanks

3

What brings you into the Valley of Death?
You get saddled with sick parents too?
My dad's like the fucking crypt keeper
I swear to God, if I have to stop in here one more time, I'm just gonna blow in his face and watch him turn to dust
I'm over it, ya know!

5

she laughs

you try to laugh too

1
No no, we're just
uh
I'm

5
you don't know how to say it

1
I got uh

2
He's helping me buy a prop

3
Ooo!

2
My character has a limp
So
I need a cane

3
You're an actor?!

2
What else would I be?

3
I love that!
Are you in a movie?!

2
No

3
Play?

2
No

3
Musical

2
Not yet

3
So what is it?

2 (*scrambling*)
Oh
It's a uh
it's a
it's a
it's a

1
It's none of your business

2
Yep

5
you all stare at each other

3
Okay!

5
and decide to move on

3
How's Liam?

2
Liam?

3
Boyfriend

2
Ooh la la

1
He's

3
Did you two ever get ahold of that real estate agent I sent you?

1
No, we

3
He's a dick, right?
I hate him
I'll send you the name of another guy I know

1
No, we decided to go at it alone

3
Omigod
In this economy?!
Have you found anything?

1
I'm still at my old place

3
But you said it was so small!

1
It was
Is, I guess
But it's plenty spacious for one

3
Then where's Liam?

5
it's quiet for a moment

3
Oh shit
I'm sorry
I

1
Don't be

3
You broke up?!

(**Actor 1** *shrugs*)

3
I'm so sorry
Liam's just

1
Yeah

3
He's just so great!

1
He is

3
Actually
No
You know what?
Fuck him
I think it's for the best

1
You don't have to say that

3
I do!
Remember when he got sick last year?
All of that time you had to take off to take care of him?
Imagine doing that for *the rest of your life*

1
Well, he's okay now, so

3
Yeah, I don't think so

66 You Will Get Sick

That kind of sick stays with you
Who knows when it would sneak up on him again

1
Margot, could you please not

3
I think you dodged a bullet
I really do
You told me all about taking care of your brother Patton

1 *and* **2**
Patrick

3
You shouldn't have to do that again
You put in your time with your brother
You don't need to take care of someone else
I mean, I'm splitting dad duty with my sisters and even three of us isn't enough
It's just too heavy for someone to

5
and then suddenly you're crying

3
Oh

5
it's not loud

it's actually very, very quiet

3
Wait

5
you can't breathe

you're crying too hard

3
What did I say?!

1
Don't be

3
You broke up?!

(**Actor 1** *shrugs*)

3
I'm so sorry
Liam's just

1
Yeah

3
He's just so great!

1
He is

3
Actually
No
You know what?
Fuck him
I think it's for the best

1
You don't have to say that

3
I do!
Remember when he got sick last year?
All of that time you had to take off to take care of him?
Imagine doing that for *the rest of your life*

1
Well, he's okay now, so

3
Yeah, I don't think so

That kind of sick stays with you
Who knows when it would sneak up on him again

1
Margot, could you please not

3
I think you dodged a bullet
I really do
You told me all about taking care of your brother Patton

1 *and* **2**
Patrick

3
You shouldn't have to do that again
You put in your time with your brother
You don't need to take care of someone else
I mean, I'm splitting dad duty with my sisters and even three of us isn't enough
It's just too heavy for someone to

5
and then suddenly you're crying

3
Oh

5
it's not loud

it's actually very, very quiet

3
Wait

5
you can't breathe

you're crying too hard

3
What did I say?!

2
Maybe you should go

3
I didn't

2
Please

3
I just
I still need to grab a shower stool for my dad

2
Okay, but could you just like
leave the immediate area?

3
Yeah
I'm
I'm sorry
I'll see you at the office, okay?

5
she leaves

and you cry

2
Do you wanna keep going?

1
I can't get up
My back is cramping

5
you can't stop crying

2
It's okay
We'll just sit here for a minute

5
she sits beside you on a display toilet seat

2 (*starts to sing Somewhere Over the Rainbow*)

1
Don't

2
Okay

5
and then it's quiet

for a very long time

1
Let's get a chair and a cane
But I want the one with the four rubber things

2
We'll get that one

10

5
she pushes you in your wheelchair

and stops outside your apartment door

2
Here

5
you try to reach into your wallet
but your arm shakes

1
Take eighty

2
We said sixty

1
I know, but I don't want it

2
This is
very generous
Thank you

5
she counts the bills

1
It's eighty

2
Nice
Almost there

1
Where?

2
What?

1
Almost where?

2
Nowhere
Do you need help with anything else?
I can tell more people that you're sick if you want
I'll only charge you fifty

1
I don't want more people knowing that I'm

2
I can take you somewhere or

1
No thanks

5
she stands in the hallway

you sit in your chair

2
Do you need help getting inside?
That's only fifteen

1
I'll be

2
Ten

1
I'll be okay

2
Well, call me if you have more money to burn

1
I will

2
You're sweating

1
Hm?

2
You're

5
she wipes your forehead with her sleeve

2
On the house

1
Thanks

2
You'll be okay?

1
Yeah
Yes

5
you peer at each other

1 (*gentle permission*)
Go home

2
Okay

1
Bye

2
Bye

1
Bye

2
Bye

5
and then she's gone

you open your door

4
There he is!

5
and find a man in your apartment

1
Hello?

5
he's tying pieces of rope to the handles of your cupboards

1
Liam?
Why are you –?

4
Hey, man, you must be you!
I'm Gavin, with Brighter Tomorrows!

1
Oh
You look like someone I know

4
I get that a lot

1
Really?

4
No

1
Okay
I told my sister not to call you guys

4
Family's like that, ya know?
She's just concerned

1
Did she let you in?

4
No need
I broke a window and climbed through

1
This is the eleventh floor

4
I know, but if I can do it, a bird can too
And birds aren't afraid of heights like I am

5
you try to stand with your new cane

4
Need some help, bud?

1
Yeah
Thanks, Liam

4
Gavin

1
Gavin
Sorry

5
you can feel his hand on your shoulders

                (**Actor 1** *can't seem to stand*)

           (**Actor 4** *helps him back into the wheelchair*)

4
It's okay
We gave it a shot

5
you can still feel it there even after he moves it away

1
I miss you

4
What's that?

1
I wish you hadn't moved back home

4
Who?

1
You, Liam

4
Gavin

1
Liam, I wanted to go with you
I did, but
but
I couldn't leave Polly behind

She's here and I'm here and now you're back home
I can't breathe, Liam

4
Gavin

1
Liam, I've been wanting to tell you that you were right about the air here
I didn't believe you
But it's
it's
Do you miss me?
I

4
You okay?

1
Hm?

4
You're sweating, bud

1
It's hot

4
I'm going to walk you through what I did, okay?

1
Sure

4
I've got your place all padded out
All your furniture has been stabilized and reinforced to the walls and floor

1
Liam

4
Gavin

In the kitchen, I've replaced your silverware with some rounded plastic cutlery
That's provided free of charge from Brighter Tomorrows, you're welcome

1
Hey, Liam

4
Gavin
The bathroom has grab bars beside the toilet, sink, and in the shower
Now a question for you

1
Liam

4
Gavin
It looks like you don't have bird insurance, which seems dicey given your situation
Are you interested in signing onto a plan with Brighter Tomorrows?
We have a

1
I can't move my arm

4
What's that?

1
I can't move it

> (**Actor 1**'s *arm is different now*)
>
> (*it's a different texture or fabric*)
>
> (*it's stuffed with hay*)

4
Fresh air will help with that!

11

5

you sit in your wheelchair
in a park
in sunlight that's starting to burn you

2

I performed a monologue from *The Wizard of Oz* in class last week, the one about wanting to go home
and I heard Student Taylor had some shit to say about it
So I cornered him after class by the vending machine and I was like, "I heard you had some shit to say, you little bitch," and I guess he doesn't know how to take a joke because he told Teacher Taylor and then she
Are you okay?
You getting hot?
C'mere

5

she holds a cool, wet towel to your forehead

your neck

your face

2

Five

5

you hand her a five-dollar bill

2

So Teacher Taylor talks to me about it and she's like, "Student Taylor is a young artist and he's still learning how to offer critique in a constructive and healthy way"
So then I'm like, "What exactly needed *critiquing*, Teacher Taylor?"
And she looks at me like I'm a giant fucking bird or something, she's just horrified, so she
Take some water

5
she tips a bottle to your lips

2
Ten

5
you hand her a ten-dollar bill

2
But she still doesn't say anything
So it's clear to me right then and there that my monologue was perfect
because there was *nothing* for them to critique
She knew it and I knew it and
You know what?
Let me just show you
Do you want to hear it?

        (**Actor 1** *tries to shake his head*)

2
It'll only cost fifteen

        (**Actor 1** *really tries to shake his head*)

2
Fuck you
It was so good

5
it's quiet for a moment

1
Hot

2
Gavin says we have to stay outside for at least thirty minutes

1
It's hot

2
He seems smart
We should listen to him

1
I told her not to
to
to call them

2
Probably a good thing she did

1
Liam took my forks

2
Who?

1
The guy

2
You mean Gavin?

1
He threw them away

2
I'm sure he just put your forks somewhere safe

1
No, he
he stole them
He

2
I don't think he stole them

1
Yes, he did
He uh
He put

2
No

1
Put

2
No

1
Put

2
No

1
Put

2
No

1
Put

2
Okay, whatever, he did

5
and then it's quiet again

1
It's hot

2
You've said

1
Hurts

2
What hurts?

1
It hurts

2
What hurts?

5
you try to point at your brain

but your arm won't let you

1
Home

5
your sight begins to tunnel

2
I know, but

5
your hearing does too

2
But Gavin told us you have to get some fresh air

1
Brain

2
What?

                    (**Actor 5**'s *voice grows tunneled*)

5
there's so much you want to say

1
I don't want my
my

5
but the words don't come

1
My

5
they get stuck in your throat

1
Brain

5
there's one

1
Brain

5
but it gets stuck on a loop

1
Brain
brain
brain

5
you push out more

1
I don't want
my brain to
to
to
be different

5
there you go

keep going

1
It
It can have my body
but *please*
please not my brain
I don't

5

you push even harder

but you're stuck on another loop

1
Don't
don't
don't
don't
Don't
don't

2
Don't *what?!*

1
Home

5
she holds the towel to your forehead

your neck

your face

2
Twenty

1
I

5
you push against her

2
Fine, fifteen

1
I want

5
you keep pushing against her

2
What's happening?

1
Home

2
Let's go

    (**Actor 5**'s *voice is even more tunneled*)

5
she begins to push your wheelchair

but you struggle against her

2
We're going back inside
You're not paying me enough to handle whatever this is
I'm getting Gavin

 (*the unintelligible sound of* **Actor 5**'s *voice trying to cut through*)

2
Let go of your wheelchair!

 (*the unintelligible sound of* **Actor 5**'s *voice trying to cut through*)

2
I'm not doing this with you
Stop!

    (**Actor 5**'s *voice is clear again*)

5
your wheelchair is accidentally tipped over

and you fall to the ground

2
Oh god!
Oh shit!

5
you begin to shake

2
Fuck!
Fuck

5
you convulse

2
Hold on
I'm

5
urine streams down your leg

2
I'm just

5
she tries to lift you back into your wheelchair
but you're shaking too hard

2
Please stop

5
you accidentally knock her to the ground

2
Jesus!

5
she peers at you

at your shaking body

2
I can't do this
I
Help!
Please!!
Somebody!!!

5
she crawls toward you

she tries to cradle your shaking head

2
Hey
Hey
It's okay
Please just
I'll be right back
I'll

5
and then she leaves

and you're alone

and maybe you believe she's coming back

or maybe you don't

12

2
That your wheelchair?

5
a woman is standing beside you

you don't know when she appeared or how

1
Callan?

2
Who?

1
Oh
You look like someone I know

2
I look like a lot of people

5
she's holding an umbrella

>（*there is no umbrella*）

5
it casts some shade over you

2
That your wheelchair?

1
Yeah

2
Nice

1
It works for me
Usually

2
I wish I would've gotten my husband one of those
Maybe the bird wouldn't have taken him

5
you peer at each other

2
Does it hurt?

1
Yes
It does

2
I'm sorry

1
Things happen
People get

5
you still can't say it

1
People get
You know
People get

2
Sick

1
Yep

5
and then it's quiet

1
It's hot

2
Where's your umbrella?

5
she's closer now

(**Actor 2** *doesn't move*)

1
I don't have one

2
There are birds

1
Yeah
Yes
You're right, there are birds

2
Giant fucking birds

1
I know

2
Birds that can eat away at you before you even know they're there

1
Birds do that, yeah

2
Wanna get under my umbrella?

1
It's hard for me to move

5
she sits beside you, holding the umbrella over your heads

(**Actor 2** *doesn't move*)

(*there is no umbrella*)

1
Thank you
That feels nice

2
Don't feed the dogs

1
Hm?

2
Dogs in the park

1
Oh
Okay

2
They're ungrateful
Inches, miles, they don't know the difference

1
Well
They're dogs

2
Don't do that
Don't defend them

1
Sorry

2
Fuck those dogs

>*(the sound of dogs barking in the distance)*

2 *(calling off)*
You heard me!

5
you try to breathe

but you can't

your lungs feel too full

2
Would you rather be a dog in a park
or a cat in a bodega?

1
A dog, I guess
The park would be better
I like open spaces

2
I'd be a dog too

1
Man's best friend

2
Or woman's

1
Yeah

2
Or person's

1
That's right

2
Would you rather watch an innocent baby bird get sick and die or a giant bird that's probably taken a lot of people?

1
The giant bird

2
Yeah, me too
Would you rather watch your mother get sick and die
or your father?

1
I've already watched my father, so I'd say him

2
You'd watch that again?

1
If it's between my mom, who's never been
You know

2
Sick

1
Yeah
Or watching my father get uh
I'd spare my mom

2
Where is she?

1
Back home
She's living with her
her new friend
Jerry
He's good to her

Which is good
She deserves good things in her life

5
she peers at you for a moment

2
Would you rather get sick and die
or watch me get sick and die?

1
I'd rather no one got

2
Yeah, but if you had to choose

1
I guess you

2
Wow

1
Sorry

2
You don't even know me

1
You asked

2
It's okay
I'd choose you too

5
a bird caws somewhere above your heads

2
I'm waiting for my husband
See if he'll fall from the sky
I don't think he will though

1
Miracles
They happen

2
I guess

1
You never know

2
We had insurance too
What a fucking joke

5
you cough

2
Sounds bad

1
No, it's not good
My O.T. says I need fresh air

2
Nothing's fresh here

1
I wish I could breathe
I can't breathe here
The city is too

2
Go home

1
I can't breathe there either
I don't dust enough

2
No, your first home
Where you come from

1
Oh
I didn't know it was that easy to tell

2
It's easy to spot the ones who grew up in the city versus the ones who fake it

1
It's been a long time since I've gone home

2
South?

1
No

2
West?

1
No

2
North?

1
Nope

2
Really?
The middle?

1
Right in the very middle

2
What was that like?

1
Spacious
You could always breathe

2
Describe it to me

1
We lived on acres and acres of land
Wheat skimming the horizon in every direction
My sister and I helped my father with the yardwork
but our brother Patrick worked the bigger plots until he got

2
Sick?

1
Yeah

2 (*a tsk*)
Everyone gets sick

1
He stopped when his body couldn't do it anymore, so I tried to help out
But I was smaller than he was, I couldn't do as much
I couldn't lift the hay
There was too much of it

5
you're suddenly covered in hay

        (**Actor 1** *is suddenly covered in hay*)

2
Like that?

5
it spills out of your clothes

1
Just like that

2
But you left

1
I know

2
You left home

1
It felt like I had too much air to breathe
Isn't that funny?
What we take for granted

2
Do you miss it?

1
I do

2
Everyone's there
They're alive and they're healthy

1
I hope so

2
It's where your boyfriend lives

1
He's not my boyfriend anymore

2
That's not what he says

1
Really?
You talk to him?

2
Of course I do, he's right here

4
Here I am

1
Liam, hi
When did you get here?

4
I've been here

1
I've been wanting to call

4
I'd love to hear from you

1
That's so nice of you to say

5
he touches you

1
I'm glad you're not
You know

4
Sick

1
Yeah

4
It's okay to say it

1
I know

4
I'm sorry that you are
Sick, I mean

1
I'm doing what I can

5
you touch him

1
Why did you leave?

4
I missed home

1
But we were trying to make this place our home

4
It wasn't right
I wasn't myself there

1
I'm not myself these days either

4
You should've come home with me

1
I wish I would have

4
I'm living near your old place

1
What's it like?

4
It's big
It's beautiful

1
I bet so

2
You should move home

1
Polly would miss me

4
Let's ask her

1
Where is she?

2
She's right here

3
Here I am

1
There you are
Polly, would you miss me if I went home?

3
Yes
But I love you enough to let you go

1
Thank you
That's just what I needed to hear

3
You could see mom

1
I want to see her

3
She's right here

2
Here I am

1
Mom
Hi

2
You've been gone so long

1
I know
I'm sorry

2
Come here

5
she holds you

1
Mom, you look good
You're not

2
Sick?
Of course I'm not
I take good care of myself

1
It doesn't matter
Things happen so quickly
One day a bird could get you

2
One day a bird could get any one of us

1
I know, but

5
a telephone begins to ring

2
You're sweating, honey

1
I'm

2
Sick
You're so sick
Stay under my umbrella

5
you hold her

1
You're all here

4
Of course we are

3
We're your family

2
Where else would we be?

1
Mom
I miss you
I want to go home
(*overcome*)
I want

                (**Actor 2** *touches* **Actor 1**)

2
I know

        (*the telephone ringing become a cacophony*)

13

3
You awake?

                  (**Actor 3** *is unseen*)

5
a telephone keeps ringing

3
Hello?

5
you're in a hospital room the color of an egg

3
About time

5
a woman peers at you over the rails of your bed

she's covered in patches of fur

you want to ask her why
but your mouth won't let you

3
You need to throw up?

5
the telephone keeps ringing

3
You should if you do

5
but then it stops

3
Don't be scared

5
you throw up lots of hay and lots of feathers

3
Okay, try not to move
You're not supposed to move until someone's seen you

5
you realize that you couldn't move even if you wanted to

>> (**Actor 1**'s *torso and other leg are different now*)
>> (*they're a different texture or fabric*)
>> (*they're stuffed with hay*)
>> (*he can only really move an arm and his head*)

1
Thanks, Polly

3
Polly?

1 (*coming to*)
Oh
I'm uh
No, I'm sorry
You sound like

3
Someone you know?

1
Polly
Polly is uh

5
it's at the tip of your tongue.

1
Polly is my

5
the distance between you and the word you're looking for feels insurmountable

1 (*growing restless*)
I'm sorry
I know this
Polly is my
uh
my

5
the woman covered in fur crawls back into a hospital bed of her own

3
Don't think too hard
That only makes it worse

5
you can hear her stirring in bed

1
I'm scared

5
you are

1
I'm scared
I'm really

3
It's okay

1
I can't do it
I

3
It's okay to be scared

5
you want to see her face

3
But you'll have to face it eventually

(**Actor 1** *tries to breathe*)

1
Does it get any better?
The

3
No

5
she stirs

3
But that's okay too

4
There he is!

(**Actor 4** *is unseen*)

5
a nurse is standing in the doorway

he's holding an armful of metallic tools
copper, steel, iron, tin

4
I'm glad to see those bright and shinies!
Did you throw up?
Looks like you threw up
Did it come easy?
Was it hard to do?
Rate the experience
Rate my service
Rate your pain
I'm sure it's fine, but ring the bell if it happens again or if

1
Sister

5
there it is

1
Polly is my *sister*

4
Sister?
No sisters
Visiting hours are over
Okay, shh for now
Let's check these vitals

5
the nurse digs through the piles of hay all around you

1
I can't breathe

4
You had a bad episode
You just threw up

1
No, I need my

4
Inhaler?
No inhaler
Let's check those arms
Let's check those legs

1
I want to go home

4
I know, but we need to keep you around a little longer
Now brain
Let's check that brain

5
the nurse tries to shove some hay back into your head

1
No!
Please
Stop!
I just
I don't want to be here!
Where's my wheelchair?!
I need it back
I want to go home!
I

4
Hey
Hey!
It's okay
Stop

5
you cry

4
I'm sorry
I

(with softness)
I know it hurts

1
I don't want to be here

4
I know it hurts being here
but it's where you need to be

5
you can't stop crying

4
I'll see if there's something we can do for the pain
Okay?

5
and then he's gone

1
Wait!

5
suddenly
the telephone rings again

you try to use your one good arm to answer it

1
Hello?

5
the receiver shakes in your hand

2
Hi

5
the connection on the telephone crackles, just a little bit

1
Wow
You're calling me

2
Thought I'd shake things up

1
How are you?

2
I'm okay
How are you?

5
you can hear her breathing

1
I'm not doing so well

2
I know

1
I have an arm though
One good arm

2
Sometimes that's enough

5
and then it's quiet

but you can still hear her breathing
so you know she's still there

1
How much money do you still need?

2
How much are you offering?

1
Will you take me home?

2
Your apartment?

1
No, my first home

2
Oh

1
I need some air to breathe

2
Is it far?

1
Yeah

2
How far?

1
Far-far
Half a country
Right in the very middle

5
there's just the sound of her breath

in and out

just like that

2
That'll cost extra

1
I don't mind

2
Are you allowed to leave?

1
No

2
That'll really cost extra

1
I know

5
and then it's quiet

for a very long time

2
Okay

1
Okay?

2
Okay

1
Okay

14

5
she takes you home

she carries you through the hospital
down a hall
past a nurse

4
Where you going?!

5
past your sister

3
I just got here!

5
into the elevator
onto the street
past an insurance salesman

4
The world is a gentler place!

5
past a dog in a park

3
It's a ruff world

5
into a cab

4
Don't get sick on the seats!

5
into an airport
into a terminal
past a flight attendant

3
I need your tickets!

5
onto a plane
into a seat between a man and woman covered in bird scratches

4
Things just happen

3
We'll make it through

5
into the air
into the clouds
past a giant crow with a husband in its beak

4
Tell my wife I miss her!

5
onto ground

onto land
right in the very middle of the country

2
Almost there

5
she carries you

and she keeps carrying you

and she doesn't stop

> *(the world folds in on itself)*
>
> *(the Big City becomes a field of wheat)*

15

2
You're here

5
you are

you're home

1
I can breathe

2
It's nice
I can see why you wanted to come back

1
It's nothing like I remembered

2
Is that okay?

1
It's fine
It's good

2
Are you glad we did this?

1
I am, yeah

2
What now?

1
I
I don't know

2
We could go back

1
No
I need to breathe some more

5
you both breathe without your inhalers

1
Thank you for bringing me home

2
It's my job

5
you want to tell her what that means to you

              (**Actor 1** *takes a breath as if to speak*)

5
but you don't

1
Here

5
you try to reach into your wallet

but you realize that it's finally happened

your one good arm

> (**Actor 1**'s *entire body is different now*)
> (*it's textured and stuffed with hay*)
> (*he looks like a scarecrow*)

1
Oh

2
It happened?

1
Yeah

2
Did it hurt?

1
No
Just
Just grab my wallet
Take whatever's in there

2
I only need enough for

> (**Actor 2** *stops*)

1
For what?

2
Nothing

1
What were you going to say?

2
Nothing
It's just
I'm
I'm buying a dress

1
A dress

2
For my audition

1
You've been saving all that money
for a dress?

2
Yeah, there's this uh
this gingham dress I saw in a consignment shop on
Sixteenth and

>   (**Actor 2** *notices* **Actor 1** *peering at her*)

2
What?

1
You don't have to lie

2
I'm not lying

1
Okay

2
I'm not

1
You blinked

2
No, I didn't

1
Then why didn't you say that before?

2
Because it's none of your business

1
A dress?

2
Yeah
A *dress*

1
Okay

2
For my audition

1
Sure

2
It's for a dress, asshole!

1
I don't care what you do with the

2
I worked hard for this money

1
I know

2
I took care of you
I don't need you to

1
I'm sorry
I'm sorry!
Just take the rest

2
No
I'm not taking more than I need
I'm taking enough to buy my dress and that's it

1
Then use the rest for a

a basket or something
I don't know
Doesn't she have a basket?

>(**Actor 2** *won't look at him*)

1
Please
I want you to have it
I don't care what you do with it
Buy a dress or don't, but please just take the money

5
it's quiet for a moment

and then she slips the money into her pocket

2
I want

>(*a moment*)

1
I know

>(*a moment*)

2
Okay

5
and then she's gone

a bird caws somewhere above you

it's tremendous, it's prehistoric
it's just right for a space this open

the sound fills up everything that has been changed inside of you

and then

>(**Actor 5** *appears*)

>(*the world changes somehow*)

(things become a little more real)

(a little more true)

5
Hey

1
Patrick

5
Welcome home, baby brother
You made it

1
Here I am

5
There you are

(**Actor 5** *"cracks an egg" on* **Actor 1***'s head*)

5
What brings you back?

1
I got

1
Huh

5
What?

1
It's still hard for me to

5
That's okay

1
I just wanted to come home

5
I'm glad you did

5
Wanna breathe together?

5
Doesn't that feel good?

1
Yeah

1
I missed breathing here

1
Was it hard telling people?
When you got

5
Nah
Not really

1
It's hard for me

5
I had to practice though
I stuffed a shirt with hay and practiced on that until I was ready

1
Say it

5
I got sick

1
Wow
Just like that

5
I got sick

1
You got

1
You got

5
I got sick

1
You got really

5
I got very sick
Things happen

1
They do, don't they?

5
You try it

1
I got sick

5
There

5
You said it

1
I got sick

5
You got sick
That's all

1
Yep

1
That's all

Coda

(a community theater)

(an audition)

(**Actor 2** *wears a gingham dress*)

2
Hello
My name is Callan
I'll be auditioning for the role of Dorothy in your production

of *The Wizard of Oz* based on the 1939 film of the same name
I have prepared for you a song and a monologue
I will begin with the song
Thank you

                (**Actor 2** *takes a breath*)

2 (*starts to sing the first lines of Somewhere Over the Rainbow*)

1

you went too low

2

I went too low
I'm sorry
I've been practicing that part because a

1

you want to say it

2

A

1

give it a try

2

A friend of mine
said that I go too low there
I think I
Can I start again?

1

you wait for a response that doesn't come

2 (*starts to sing the first lines of Somewhere Over the Rainbow*)

1

you went too low

2

Fuck
I know, I heard it

I heard it that time
I'm just

1

you're feeling overwhelmed

2

Hello
My name is Callan
I'll be auditioning for the role of Dorothy in your production
of *The Wizard of Oz* based on the 1939 film of the same name
I have prepared for you a song and a monologue
I will begin with the monologue
Thank you

1

you breathe

you breathe it all in

2

I will now perform a monologue written by a

(*a moment*)

1

it's okay

you don't have to say it

2

Written by some guy I met

The End